How to Draw
CATS & KITTENS

Learn to draw **20** different kitties, step by easy step, shape by simple shape!

Illustrated by Diana Fisher

Walter Foster
Jr.

Getting Started

When you look closely at the drawings in this book, you'll notice that they're made up of basic shapes, such as circles, triangles, and rectangles. To draw any feline, just start with simple shapes as you see here. It's easy and fun!

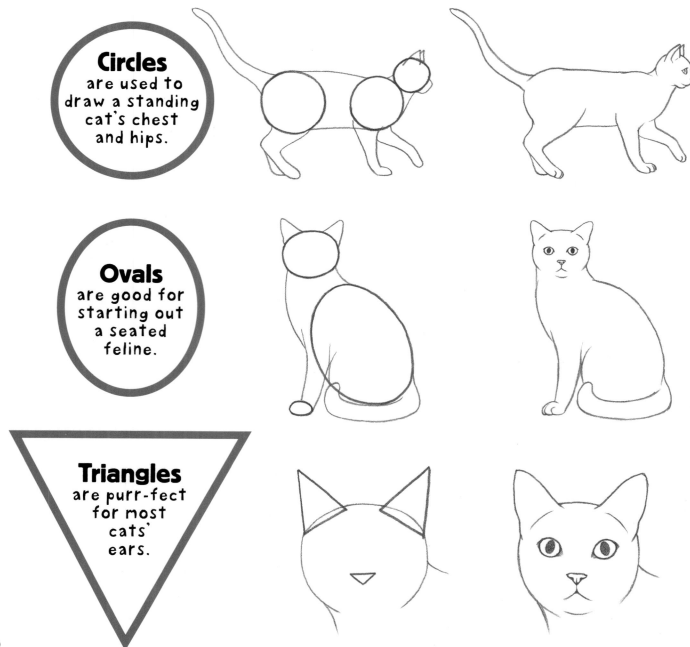

Circles are used to draw a standing cat's chest and hips.

Ovals are good for starting out a seated feline.

Triangles are purr-fect for most cats' ears.

Tips

There's more than one way to bring furry felines to life on paper—you can use crayons, markers, or pencils. Just be sure you have plenty of good natural hues, such as black, brown, orange, pink, and green.

Pencils

Crayons

Markers

Persian Cat

The popular Persian is known for its long, luxurious coat. But its face, neck, body, and legs are all short—so is its bushy tail!

5

fun fact

Persians require a lot of grooming! They have longer, thicker coats than any other domestic cats— their topcoat can be up to 5 inches (12.7 cm) long!

6

Egyptian Mau

The Mau cat sports both spots and stripes! And this social kitty has a reputation for being playful as well as graceful.

British Shorthair

The best words to describe this feline are large and round! And circles and ovals are the purr-fect shapes for drawing this quiet cat!

Selkirk Rex Kitten

Selkirk Rex kittens often have shaggy, rumpled-looking fur. When they reach adulthood, their wavy locks become curly coats.

fun fact

The Selkirk Rex is a natural breed that was discovered in the United States in 1987. Like the Cornish Rex and the Devon Rex, this breed has a curly coat. But with its stronger, rounder body, it looks very different from its fellow "Rex" cats!

Abyssinian Kitten

Abys are short-haired cats with strong bodies—and stronger personalities! These curious kitties are intelligent and outgoing.

fun fact

The first documented Aby came from Ethiopia in 1868—but many believe that this elegant breed is a descendant of the cats of ancient Egypt! The mummified cats found in Pharaohs' tombs are similar to today's Abyssinian in many ways.

Cornish Rex

with a wavy coat, a wiry body, a whiplike tail, and prominent "bat" ears, the cornish Rex is easy to notice and hard to forget!

5

6

7

8

fun fact

It may look like something from outer space, but the Cornish Rex is actually named after a bunny! The owner of the first Cornish Rex named the breed for its plush coat, which feels similar to the velveteen coat of the Rex breed of rabbits.

Maine Coon

It's easy to see where the gentle giant of the cat world got its name! This Maine native has a bushy, ringed tail—like a raccoon's!

fun fact

The Maine Coon is the oldest American breed and the first native American show cat! Although it now places second in breed popularity, it comes first in size. Some males weigh 20 pounds (9 kg) or more, and this Yankee cat is four times the size of the Singapura, the smallest cat breed.

Ragdoll

This soft, fluffy cat is so relaxed that it flops like a rag doll when picked up! An affectionate breed, Ragdolls love to cuddle.

Manx

Lots of cats have short tails or no tails, but the manx is the only one specifically bred to be tail-free.

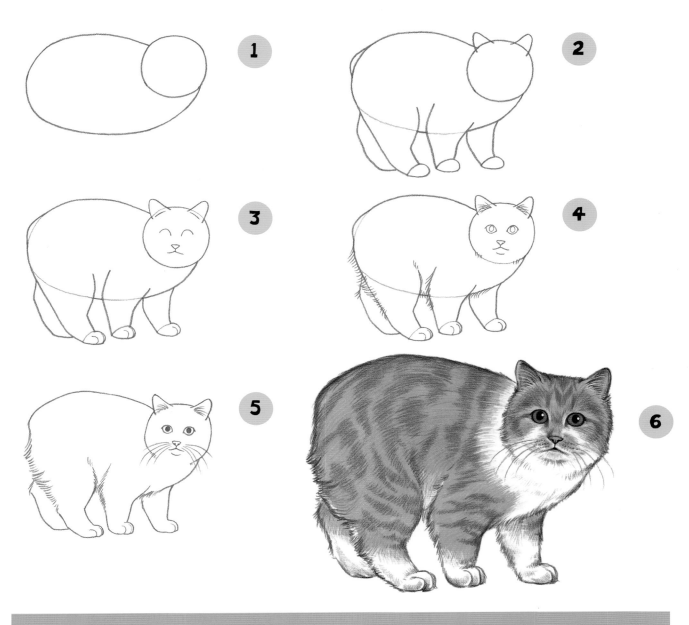

1 2 3 4 5 6

fun fact

The Manx is known for not having a tail, but some have normal-length tails (known as "longies") and some have short tails (known as "stumpies.")

Turkish Angora

This beautiful breed has a slender body, a long neck, a wedge-shaped head, and sometimes two eyes that are different hues. The Turkish Angora is playful and devoted!

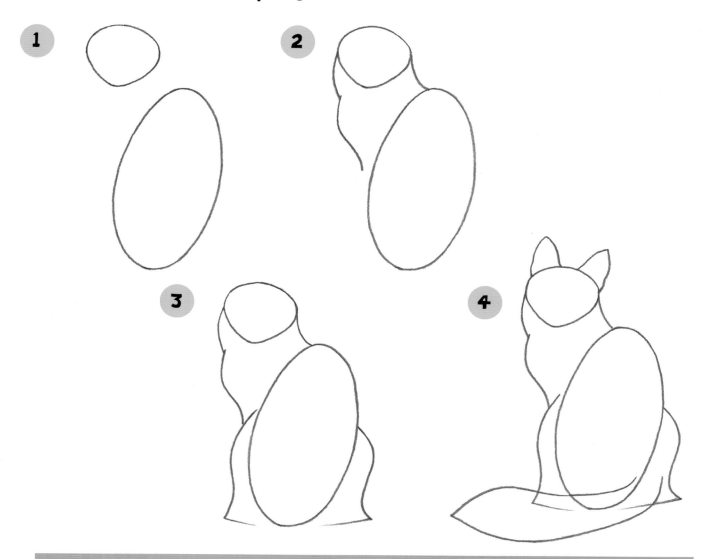

fun fact

The Turkish Angora is one of the national treasures of its homeland, Turkey. It was the first long-haired cat to be brought to Europe and was the darling of European aristocracy in the 1700s. But the breed lost popularity, and these cats would be extinct today if not for the Turkish zoos that saved them!

Russian Blue

Quiet-loving Blues can happily sit still for hours. To draw this cat in its comfy pose, begin with marshmallow shapes for its head and body.

fun fact

As you might guess from its name, the Russian Blue comes from Russia, where it was discovered by the British about 200 years ago. This breed has had many names in the past, including "Russian Shorthair," "Maltese Blue," "Archangel Blue," and "Foreign Blue."

American Curl

The curl is the only breed with ears that curl backward. It's a good thing this friendly feline loves attention!

Norwegian Forest Cats

The Wegie is a furry feline with a thick, heavy coat of fur. Its mane and tail are fluffy, and its triangular ears are straight and tall!

5

6

7

fun fact

Vikings (Scandinavian seafarers) liked to have cats on their ships to fight pest populations, so they picked up mousers at ports around the world. They brought the first cats to Norway around the year 1000. Cold Nordic winters suited cats with sturdy builds and thick coats, so these imported cats eventually developed into a new breed: Norwegian Forest Cats.

Scottish Fold

with unusual flat, folded ears, a round head, and golden eyes, the Scottish Fold looks like the feline version of an owl!

fun fact

Scottish Folds aren't bred with other Folds because their kittens can have crippling skeletal problems. To keep this breed healthy, Folds are mated with Scottish Straights (cats from the same bloodline without folded ears) and American or British Shorthairs.

Birman Kitten

The round white paws on this breed—also known as "The Sacred cat of Burma"—distinguish it from other varieties.

Traditional Siamese

This "old-fashioned" cat looks different than the triangular-headed Siamese, but both breed types are talkative and attention-loving.

fun fact

Siamese cats are very "talkative" and opinionated. "We are Siamese if you please. We are Siamese if you don't please," from Disney's *Lady and the Tramp* expresses their personality perfectly.

Japanese Bobtail

Most members of this centuries-old bobtail breed display a patched calico pattern called "mi-ke," which the Japanese consider lucky.

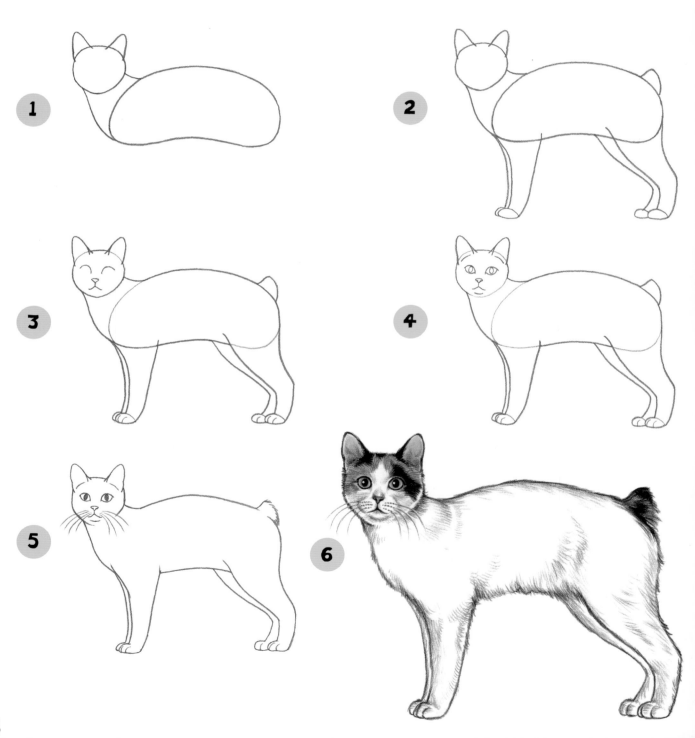

Sphynx

The huge, triangular ears of this hairless cat are hard to miss! And its wrinkled skin, wide-set eyes, and large paws also draw attention.

fun fact

The Sphynx is the only modern hairless cat breed—
but it isn't the first of its kind.
The ancient Aztecs also kept hairless cats;
unfortunately, the Aztec breed is now extinct.

Somali

The wild-looking Somali is a long-haired version of the Abyssinian. This feline's coat is thickest at the ruff, haunches, and tail.

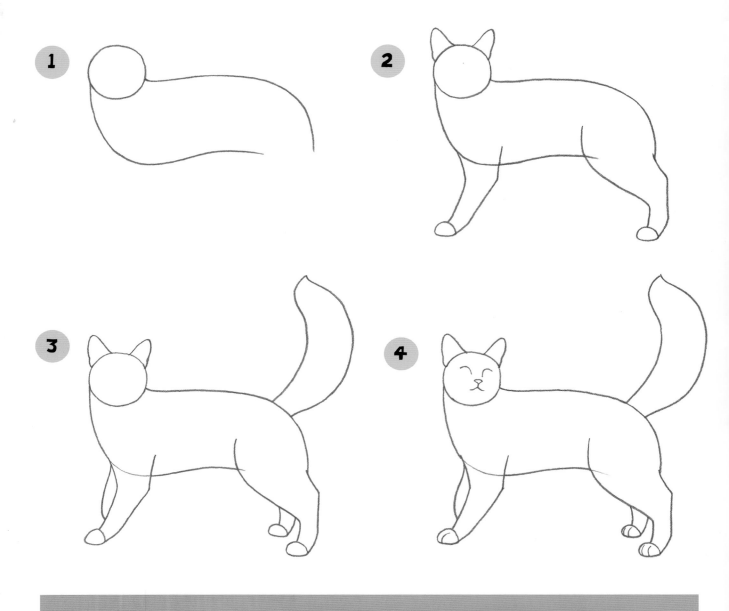

fun fact

The Somali's body shape, reddish-brown fur, and full coat combine to make this cat look like another animal altogether. So it should come as no surprise that the Somali's nickname is "fox cat."

Korat

In Thailand, this shiny-coated cat is considered a symbol of good luck! The breed is also known for being vocal and affectionate.